N

in English

3

*Third Edition*

Michael Walker

**Addison-Wesley Publishing Company**
Reading, Massachusetts • Menlo Park, California • New York
Don Mills, Ontario • Wokingham, England • Amsterdam • Bonn
Singapore • Sydney • Tokyo • Madrid • San Juan

**A Publication of the World Language Division**

**Director of Product Development:** Judith Bittinger
**Project Director:** Elinor Chamas
**Editorial:** Kathleen Sands Boehmer
**Manufacturing/Production:** James W. Gibbons
**Design:** Jeff Kelly
**Illustrations:** Allan Eitzen, Walter Fournier, Akhito Shirakawa, Randy Verougstraete
**Art Direction:** Publishers' Graphics

**Photo Credits:** p. 1, Erich Hartmann/Magnum Photos, Inc.; p. 8, NASA; p. 9. Marc Riboud/Magnum Photos, Inc.; p. 13, N.Y. Convention & Visitors Bureau; p. 21, © Abbas/Magnum Photos, Inc.; p. 25, John Hancock Mutual Life Insurance Company; p. 33, Photo by Henri Cartier-Bresson/Magnum Photos, Inc.; p. 37, Jean-Claude Lejeune/Stock, Boston; p. 45, © BILD Service; p. 49, © Charles Gatewood/Stock, Boston; p. 54, © Barbara Alper/Stock, Boston, © Doreen E. Pugh/Photo Researchers, Inc., © Frank Siteman/Stock, Boston; p. 56, Robert Frerck, Woodfin Camp; p. 57, © Brent Jones; p. 61, © Allen Green/Photo Researchers; p. 68, Josephus Daniels; p. 69, American Red Cross; p. 73, Arizona Office of Tourism Photo; p. 81, William H. Regan, Los Alamos National Laboratory Public Information Office; p. 85, © Stedt/Photo Researchers; p. 90, Puerto Rico Tourism Development Co.; p. 92, Area Research Center, Murphy Library; p. 93, Margaret Nelson; p. 97, © J.R. Holland/Stock, Boston; p. 104, Van Nostrand Photos, Photo Researchers; p. 105, © Leonard Freed/Magnum Photos, Inc.; p. 109, © Elizabeth Hamlin/Stock, Boston; p. 116, H. Rogers, Monkmeyer; p. 117, Kulvur/Magnum Photos, Inc.
**Additional art credit:** pp. 20, 54, Deborah Pinkney; p. 80, Doron Ben-Ami
**Acknowledgements:** p. 70, "Sunning" from A WORLD TO KNOW by James S. Tippett. Copyright 1933 Harper & Brothers; renewed 1961 by Martha K. Tippett. Reprinted with permission of Harper & Row, Publishers; p. 118, "Why Nobody Pets the Lion at the Zoo" from THE REASON FOR THE PELICAN by John Ciardi. Copyright © 1959 by John Ciardi. Published by J. B. Lippincott Company.

ISBN: 0-201-53508-4
    4 5 6 7 8 9 10-VH-99 98 97 96 95 94

# Introduction

NEW HORIZONS IN ENGLISH is a communication-based, six-level, basal series planned and written to make the learning of English as a second language effective and rewarding. Stimulating opportunities to practice listening, speaking, reading, and writing skills develop independence and confidence in the use of English. Thoughtfully chosen vocabulary gives students the words they need to communicate in their new language in a variety of situations; carefully paced introduction of grammatical and structural concepts helps insure a strong foundation of communication skills.

Important to every learner is a sense of achievement, a feeling that he or she has successfully accomplished the tasks presented. Motivation, the desire to learn, is equally important. NEW HORIZONS IN ENGLISH is written to satisfy both needs: to provoke, through selection of topics, vocabulary, and illustrations, a genuine interest in learning more, and to pace and schedule material in such a way that achievement and mastery are facilitated.

The language used in NEW HORIZONS IN ENGLISH is contemporary and relevant. Most important, it is English that students can and will use outside the classroom. Natural exchanges and dialogues arise from the real-life situations that form unit themes. New to this edition is the addition of literature, with selections that will increase students' enjoyment of the language. Also, students will be challenged by the "Fast Track" pages in which new and varied material is presented.

The emphasis on speaking and listening, with meaning always paramount, means that oral communicative competence develops early and is broadened and deepened as students move through the series. Parallel development of reading and writing skills promotes competence in other communication areas at the same time.

Dialogues and readings from the texts, and many of the exercises, are recorded on the optional tape cassette program, which provides models of American pronunciation and intonation.

A complete program to build communicative competence, NEW HORIZONS IN ENGLISH provides motivation, mastery, and a sense of achievement. Every student—and every teacher—needs the feeling of pride in a job well done. NEW HORIZONS IN ENGLISH, with its unbeatable formula for classroom success, insures that this need will be filled.

# Contents

1
Were you at the concert last night?
No, I was having dinner at the White House.
WASHINGTON DC
TOUR USA

# Partner Practice

—Where are you going tonight?
—I'm going to the **library.**
—Do you have a good time there?
—Oh, yes. I really like the **books** there.

1. **video store**
   **movies**

2. **museum**
   **art**

3. **concert hall**
   **music**

4. **mall**
   **stores**

5. **theater**
   **actors**

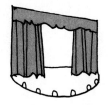 

6. **computer store**
   **software**

—Did you go to the **movies** last night?

—Yes, I did.
—No, I didn't.

1.

2.

3.

4.

—What were you wearing at the party last night?

—I was wearing my new **jeans**.

1.

2.

3.

4.

5.

6.

7.

8.

9.

**MEMORY BANK**

| 1. shirt | 2. skirt | 3. sweater |
| 4. jacket | 5. shoes | 6. suit |
| 7. boots | 8. dress | 9. blouse |

| | | 1. | 2. |
|---|---|---|---|
| I | am (not) . . .<br>was (not) . . . | | |
| You<br>We<br>They | are (not) . . .<br>were (not) . . . | 3. | 4. |
| He<br>She | is (not) . . .<br>was (not) . . . | | |
| I<br>You<br>We<br>They | like (don't like) . . .<br>liked (didn't like) . . . | 5. | 6. |
| He<br>She | likes (doesn't like) . . .<br>liked (didn't like) . . . | 7. | 8. |

MEMORY BANK

| | |
|---|---|
| 1. working | 2. sleeping |
| 3. playing | 4. eating |
| 5. dancing | 6. studying |
| 7. reading | 8. shopping |

## ON YOUR OWN

Work with a friend. Tell what you were doing yesterday, what you like, and what you don't like. Write down what your friend says.

Hi, there. My name is Nina. I'm 15, and I'm still a student. My brother is 25. He's a teacher. He likes playing golf. I can't play golf, and I don't think it's very interesting. I like playing table tennis. We have a table at home, so I practice a lot. My brother doesn't like table tennis. We were playing last night after dinner. He wasn't playing well, but *I* was. I was having a good time, but he wasn't! He doesn't like losing!

| | |
|---|---|
| 1. Hi, Nina. Are you 14? | No, I'm not. |
| 2. Are you 15? | Yes, I am. |
| 3. Is your brother a pilot? | No, he isn't. |
| 4. Is he a teacher? | Yes, he is. |
| 5. Does he like playing golf? | Yes, he does. |
| 6. Does he like playing table tennis? | No, he doesn't. |
| 7. Do you like playing golf? | No, I don't. |
| 8. Do you like playing table tennis? | Yes, I do. |
| 9. Can you practice at home? | Yes, I can. |
| 10. Did you and your brother play today? | No, we didn't. |
| 11. Did you play last night? | Yes, we did. |
| 12. Was your brother good? | No, he wasn't. |
| 13. Were you good? | Yes, I was! |

# Read & Understand

## CLOTHES MAKE THE MAN

My name is Frank Novak. I like to dance and bowl, so last Saturday I decided to go to the Bowl and Rock.

I was wearing my new suit, but all the other people were wearing slacks or jeans and sport shirts. I felt overdressed and silly. Everyone was dancing or bowling and having a good time. I asked a pretty blond to dance. She just looked at me and walked away. I walked around for a while and I listened to the music. Then I walked home early.

I'm going to go again next Saturday, though — after I go shopping for some new clothes.

1. Where did Frank decide to go?
2. What was he wearing?
3. What were the other people wearing?
4. How did Frank feel?
5. What was everyone doing?
6. Who did he ask to dance?
7. Did she dance with him?
8. What did Frank do then?
9. Is he going back? Why?

Tell Frank what to wear!

## HOW ABOUT *YOU*?
What do you like doing? Is what you wear really important?

# Conversations

ANNA: Hi, Joe. Are you shopping for new clothes?

JOE: Yes, I am. Look at these { boots. / jeans. / running shoes.

ANNA: I like them. Are they expensive?

JOE: No, they're not. They're only { $15.00. / $18.00. / $42.00.

ANNA: Why don't you buy a { shirt / tie / belt } too?

JOE: Good idea. How about this one?

ANNA: It's nice — and only { $9.00. / $13.50. / $11.00.

JOE: Wait a minute, and we can have { coffee / a pizza / tea } together.

ANNA: Oh, thanks, but I can't wait.

I have to go to the { library / post office / museum } before { 4:30. / 5:00. / 5:15.

JOE: See you later, then.

ANNA: So long.

# Career Corner

*Jack Bellows is an astronomer —
an expert on the planets and
stars. Career Corner is interviewing him.*

CC   Are other planets like
earth, Mr. Bellows?

JB   Well, in size, Venus is
almost a twin. But the
temperature on the
surface is over 500 de-
grees.

CC   Five hundred degrees,
Fahrenheit? Wow!

JB   And the winds on Venus
blow over 300 miles per
hour.

CC   What about Mars?

JB   Mars has no water and no
oxygen. The temperature

at noon is never above 50
degrees. In winter, tem-
peratures can drop to 200
degrees below zero!

CC   So we are alone in the
universe?

JB   I don't know. There are
lots of stars like our sun.
There may be other
planets out there like our
earth. We may have
brothers in space . . . but
we haven't found them
yet. Venus is too close to
the sun to support life.
Mars is too far away. The
earth is in just the right
place.

CC   Well, there's no place like
home!

**Venus**

# Picture This!

Work in small groups. Use your imagination as you answer the questions. Then write about the picture on your own.

1. What country do these people live in?
2. How are the people dressed?
3. Can you read any of the signs?
4. What kind of vehicles are on the street?
5. Where are the people going?
6. Look at the man in the uniform. What is his job?

# The Dog and the Bone

One day, a dog was out taking a walk. He was carrying a bone in his mouth. As he was walking across a bridge, he looked down at the river.

The dog saw his own reflection in the water. But he thought it was another dog. "There's a dog looking up at me," he thought. "And he has a bone, too. That bone looks bigger than my bone. I'll frighten that dog and grab his bone away."

The dog began to bark. And, of course, as soon as he opened his mouth, he dropped his bone. It fell into the river and floated away. The dog had been very silly.

*What's the moral of this fable?*

# Fast Track: *Read and Find Out*

## METALS

Silver is the most common precious metal. It is lighter than gold. We use half the silver we mine on photographic film.

*   *   *

We use aluminum for beer and soft drink cans. It is a very light metal and it is replacing steel in such things as aircraft, cars, cameras, window-frames and bicycles.

*   *   *

Platinum is the most expensive metal in the world. Unlike silver, it will not tarnish. We use it in jewelry for mounting precious stones.

*   *   *

Some streams and rivers carry gold particles after running over rocks containing the precious metal. In the old days, they put the fleece of a sheep into the stream. The wool of the fleece trapped the tiny pieces of metal.

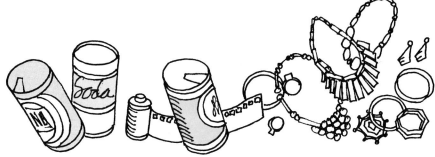

### Which is correct?

1. a) Gold is heavier than silver.
   b) Silver is heavier than gold.
   c) Silver is half as light as gold.

2. a) We use steel instead of aluminum to make soft drink cans.
   b) We often use aluminum instead of steel.
   c) We use aluminum instead of silver.

3. a) Platinum and silver tarnish.
   b) Silver, unlike platinum, tarnishes.
   c) Platinum, unlike silver, tarnishes.

# Listen & Understand

1. a  b  c

2. a  b  c

3. a  b  c

4. a  b  c

5.

Listen and write down:
a) what he's wearing
b) when he's going
c) what he likes to do

# 2

I'm starving! I want to stop for a hot dog over there.
You're always starving.
NEW YORK
TOUR USA

# Partner Practice

—Please pass the **sugar**.
—Here you are. Do you want some **eggs**?
—No thanks. I'm having some **cereal**.
—How about **a cup of coffee**?
—No, I'm having **a glass of milk**.

1.  toast
2.  syrup
3.  milk
4.  butter
5.  jelly
6.  salt and
    pepper

7.  sausage
8.  pancakes
9.  bananas
10. cheese
11. bacon
12. fruit

13. a cup of hot
    chocolate
14. a glass of
    juice
15. a cup of tea

Do you ever have [eggs / cereal / tea] for breakfast?

often
always

Yes, often.

Yes, every day.

Yes, always.

No, not often.

No, never.

1. Do you often have a big lunch?
2. Do you often drink tea?
3. Do you see Jane often?
4. Do you ever eat cake for breakfast?
5. Do you ever watch TV in the afternoon?
6. Do you always get to school on time?
7. Do you always drink your coffee black?
8. Do you always study your lessons?
9. Do you ever go to the health club?
10. Do you always watch your weight?

## ON YOUR OWN

*Now ask a friend if he or she:*

1. always has a big dinner.
2. always drinks coffee for breakfast.
3. often sees his/her grandmother.
4. ever eats pancakes for breakfast.
5. often listens to the radio.
6. often gets to school late.
7. often goes to the movies.

Does your father have [pancakes, sandwich, fruit, cheese, milk] for breakfast?

Yes, always. / often. / usually. / sometimes.

No, never. / hardly ever. / not usually.

1. Does your father get up early?
2. Does your mother get up late?
3. Does your best friend get dressed before breakfast?
4. Does your sister like black coffee?
5. Does your mother make your breakfast?
6. Does your brother have cheese for breakfast?

## ON YOUR OWN

*Ask a friend if his or her:*

1. mother gets up early.
2. father likes working.
3. sister has tea for breakfast.
4. best friend likes eggs for breakfast.
5. brother gets up late every day.
6. mother often goes to a museum.

Does your mother get up early?

| | | | | | |
|---|---|---|---|---|---|
| Did | you | play | | last summer? | Yes, every day. often. |
| | your best friend | | | | No, never. not often. hardly ever. |

1. Did you help your mother last week?
2. Did you work last summer?
3. Did your friend speak English last year?
4. Did your friend dance at a disco last year?
5. Did you live in Canada last year?
6. Did you study hard last year?

## ON YOUR OWN

*Ask a friend if he or she:*

Did you work last summer?

1. worked last summer.
2. played tennis last year.
3. lived in Mexico last summer.
4. studied hard last week.
5. watched TV last month.

## MEMORY BANK

baseball  backgammon  drums  tennis  chess  piano

# Read & Understand

A BALANCED DIET

    I think it is very silly to eat too much. I try to watch my weight. Of course, I like a small breakfast. I usually start with a glass of orange juice. Then I have one or two pieces of toast with jelly and a cup of hot chocolate. After that I have one or two eggs, some bacon and sausage. I always have a cup of tea with milk and sugar. Sometimes I have cornflakes with a banana on top. I usually finish my breakfast with a cup of black coffee. If I'm still a little hungry, I often have pancakes with butter and syrup. I have a good breakfast every morning.

    That's all I eat. I never eat lunch, and I never have dinner. If I have dinner, I can't sleep. It's silly to overeat!

HOW ABOUT *YOU?*

    What do you eat for breakfast, lunch, and dinner?

# Conversations

DAN: Good morning.

FRAN: Good morning, sir. What would you like?

DAN: Some juice, please.

FRAN: Orange?
Grapefruit?
Apple?
. . . . ?

DAN: . . . . . .

FRAN: Something else?

DAN: Eggs and toast, please.

FRAN: Scrambled?   White?
Fried?   Wheat?
Poached?   Rye?
. . . . ?   . . . . ?

DAN: . . . . . . . .

FRAN: And to drink?
Coffee?   Hot chocolate?
Tea?   Herb tea?
Milk?   . . . . . .

DAN: . . . . . . . .

# Career Corner

*Dennis Fong is a nutritionist— an expert on food. He has a TV program called "You Are What You Eat." Career Corner is interviewing him.*

CC  Is it true that food affects the way we feel?

DF  Absolutely. Too many sweets can make you moody or bad-tempered. They are also bad for your teeth.

CC  What do you suggest instead?

DF  Honey instead of sugar. Fresh fruit drinks instead of soft drinks.

CC  What else can we do to be healthier?

DF  Cut down on artificial preservatives. Eat food high in fiber, low in fat. Give up salt.

CC  Does that mean no more hamburgers, french fries, and milk shakes?

DF  Cut down on them if you can't cut them out.

CC  I can't!

DF  Yes, you can. You'll be a healthier, happier person. Eat right from the four food groups: dairy, fruits and vegetables, grain, and meat.

# Picture This!

Work in small groups. Use your imagination as you answer the questions. Then write about the picture on your own.

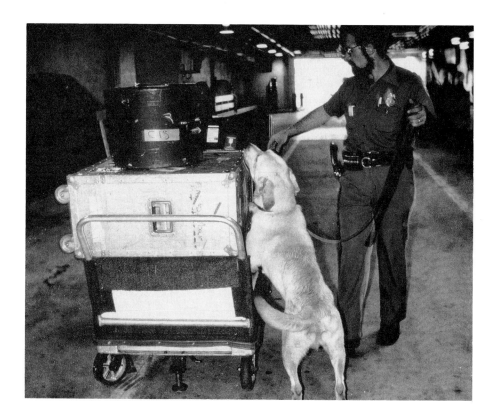

1. What is happening here?
2. What is this dog looking for?
3. Where do you think this scene is?
4. How did the dog learn to do this?
5. Why are dogs trained to do this?

# Oath of Friendship

*Shang ya!*
I want to be your friend
For ever and ever without break or decay.
When the hills are all flat
And the rivers are all dry.
When it lightens and thunders in winter,
When it rains and snows in summer,
When Heaven and Earth mingle—
Not till then will I part from you.

*Anonymous*
China, 1st century B.C.

# Fast Track: *Read and Find Out*

## FISHING

Of all the fish we catch in the world, we eat only three quarters of it. The rest goes to glue, soap, margarine, pet food and fertilizer.

\* \* \*

Fishermen usually freeze fish they catch at sea. Back in port, they defrost the fish, fillet it and sell it as fresh fish.

\* \* \*

Over ninety-five percent of fish caught is in the northern hemisphere. Thus, only about five percent of all fish caught is from south of the equator.

\* \* \*

The Japanese are the world champion fish eaters. They eat twice as much fish as their closest rivals, the Scandinavians, and five times as much fish as the average American.

\* \* \*

The Russian sturgeon is the most expensive fish in the world. The eggs of the female sturgeon are called caviar.

## Which is correct?

1. a) We use fish to make margarine.
   b) We eat all the fish we catch.
   c) We do not use 25% of the fish we catch.

2. a) We catch most fish south of the equator.
   b) We catch most fish on or just north of the equator.
   c) We catch most fish north of the equator.

3. a) Americans eat five times as much fish as the Scandinavians.
   b) Scandinavians eat five times as much fish than the Americans.
   c) The Americans do not eat as much fish as the Japanese.

# Pronunciation

**I.**

| | | | |
|---|---|---|---|
| chess | cheap | chase | chicken |
| sandwich | church | change | watch |
| which | children | chair | catch |
| teacher | cheese | chubby | charge |

The children were playing chess in the kitchen.

The teacher charged a cheap chair.

Charles is chasing a chubby chicken!

The girl was eating a cheese sandwich and watching TV.

**II.**

| | | | |
|---|---|---|---|
| shorts | push | short | vacation |
| fish | shoe | English | chef |
| crash | shave | ship | cash |
| shirt | brush | sugar | splash |

My father doesn't like to shave on vacation.

She asked the chef to make fish.

Bill is brushing his new English shoes.

I'm going to wear shorts and a new shirt on the ship.

**III.** She washed the children's shorts and shirts.

He charged fish, cheese, chicken and meat sandwiches.

Dan was pushing his car, and it crashed into a tree!

I shave every morning, and then I wash my face.

The children are eating big dishes of peaches and cream.

Charles is shopping for a chair for the kitchen.

I don't have the cash for a vacation on a ship.

I want a chicken sandwich and tea with sugar, please.

# Partner Practice

—What time do you get up?

—At

—Every day?

—No, I get up at  on **Sunday**.

**1. Mon.**　　　　　**2. Tues.**　　　　　**3. Wed.**

**4. Thurs.**　　　　**5. Fri.**　　　　　**6. Sat.**

—How do you get to work?
—By **bus**.
—Every day?
—No, sometimes I ride with Mike.

**1.** 　　**2.** 　　**3.**

**4.** 　　**5.** 　　**6.**

MEMORY BANK

| | | |
|---|---|---|
| 1. train | 2. scooter | 3. bicycle |
| 4. taxi | 5. car | 6. motorcycle |

**What's Kate doing now?**  She's washing her face. She washes her face every morning.

1. What's Bill doing now?  He's shaving. He shaves every morning.

2. What's Jill doing now? He's brushing her teeth. She brushes her teeth every morning.

3. What's Peter doing now?  He's combing his hair. He combs his hair every morning.

4. What's Lydia doing now?  She's ironing a dress. She irons a dress every morning.

5. What's Frank doing now?  He's drying his hair. He dries his hair every morning.

6. What's Pat doing now?  She's curling her hair. She curls her hair every morning.

| What are they doing now? |  | They're making coffee. They make coffee every morning. |

1. What are they doing now?

They're making the beds. They make the beds every morning.

2. What are they doing now?

They're feeding the dog. They feed the dog every morning.

3. What are they doing now?

They're walking the dog. They walk the dog every morning.

4. What are they doing now?

They're doing the dishes. They do the dishes every morning.

5. What are they doing now?

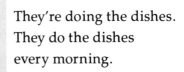

They're emptying the trash. They empty the trash every morning.

6. What are they doing now?

They're jogging. They jog every morning.

**Does she watch TV every day?**  **No, but she's watching TV now.**

1. Does he take a shower every day?  No, but he's taking a shower now.

2. Does she vacuum the rugs every day? No, but she's vacuuming the rugs now.

3. Does he do the dishes every day? 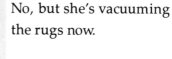 No, but he's doing the dishes now.

**Do they walk the dog every day?** No, but they're walking the dog now.

1. Do they clean the house every day?  No, but they're cleaning the house now.

2. Do they make the beds every day?  No, but they're making the beds now.

3. Do they jog every day?  No, but they're jogging now.

# Read & Understand

MORNING ROUTINES

Anita usually gets up at 7:15 every morning. She takes a shower and gets dressed. She has breakfast at about 7:35. She leaves home at the same time her father does—ten past eight. Her father drives to work, but Anita catches the bus.

Anita walks to the bus stop. It takes her five minutes. She waits for the bus. The buses come often—about every ten minutes. Anita rides the bus for twenty minutes or so. When she gets off, she often walks in the park for a quarter of an hour. Then it's time to go to work. Anita works in a store.

1. When does Anita get up?
2. What does she do first?
3. What time does she have breakfast?
4. How does she get to work?
5. How often do the buses come?
6. Where does she often walk?
7. Why do you think Anita walks a lot?

ON YOUR OWN

Talk or write about what you usually do every morning. Then have some fun. Pretend you can do anything you want in the morning. What's your morning like now?

# Conversations

BOB: Hello, Betty? This is Bob.

BETTY: Hi, Bob.

BOB: Can you give me a ride to $\begin{cases} \text{work} \\ \text{school} \\ \text{town} \end{cases}$ this morning?

BETTY: Sure, but what's wrong with *your* car?

BOB: My $\begin{cases} \text{wife} \\ \text{son} \\ \text{daughter} \end{cases}$ wants it today.

BETTY: Oh. Where's $\begin{cases} \text{she} \\ \text{he} \end{cases}$ going?

BOB: To the $\begin{cases} \text{university.} \\ \text{supermarket. There's a special} \\ \text{museum.} \end{cases}$ $\begin{cases} \text{class} \\ \text{show} \\ \text{sale} \end{cases}$ today.

BETTY: What time can you be ready?

BOB: In $\begin{cases} \text{half an hour.} \\ \text{twenty minutes.} \\ \text{ten minutes.} \end{cases}$

BETTY: Fine. I'm just $\begin{cases} \text{drying my hair} \\ \text{ironing a dress} \\ \text{making my lunch} \end{cases}$ now.

See you in $\begin{cases} \text{twenty minutes.} \\ \text{half an hour.} \\ \text{ten minutes.} \end{cases}$

# Career Corner

*Maria Perez works for a travel agency. She is a tour guide. She has been to Europe more than twenty times. Career Corner is interviewing her.*

**CC** What's your favorite tour, Ms. Perez?

**MP** That's hard to say. I like the tours in France. I like the tours through Italy and Germany, too.

**CC** What do you have to do on a tour?

**MP** First I meet everybody at the airport. I get all the tourists and their bags on the bus. Then I take them to their hotel.

**CC** Then can you relax?

**MP** Oh, no. I'm in charge of every day of the tour. I get the tourists on the bus. I describe the sights. I make sure the meals are good. I help the tourists with their shopping. If a tourist gets sick, I call a doctor. If a tourist gets lost, I have to find him or her.

**CC** So you're busy twenty-four hours a day?

**MP** Just about. But I love my job.

**CC** What languages do you speak, Ms. Perez?

**MP** Well, Spanish and English, of course. I also speak French fairly well.

**CC** It sounds like you are happy in your career.

**MP** I'm very happy. If you like people, and if you like to travel, being a tour guide is the best!

# Picture This!

Work in small groups. Use your imagination as you answer the questions. Then write about the picture on your own.

1. Where are these people?
2. How old are they?
3. Do they work, or do they go to school?
4. What are they watching? A rock star? Clowns? A soccer game? What?
5. Who are they waving at?
6. Pretend you're one of the people in this picture. Talk about yourself.

# The Boy Who Cried Wolf

Once, a shepherd boy was watching his flock of sheep. He got bored, and decided to have some fun.

"Help, help!" he cried. "Wolf! Wolf! The wolves are attacking my sheep."

The people in the village came running to help. The shepherd boy laughed and said, "There are no wolves. I was just fooling." The villagers went back to their work.

But the shepherd boy cried "Wolf! Wolf!" three more times. Three more times, the villagers came running. And three more times the boy laughed. He thought it was a great joke. The villagers did not.

Soon after, some wolves really did come. The shepherd boy cried "Wolf! Wolf!" But the villagers didn't come. The boy ran to the village.

"Help! The wolves are attacking my sheep!" he cried. "You won't fool us again." said the villagers. And so the boy lost all of his sheep.

*What is the moral of this fable?*

# Fast Track: *Read and Find Out*

## FARMING

Goats and sheep were the first tame animals. They kept them in Iran and Iraq about 8500 B.C. for milk and meat.

\* \* \*

In Australia there are more than three times as many sheep as people. The largest sheep station is in South Australia and is about one million hectares (2.5 million acres). It is bigger than the island of Cyprus.

\* \* \*

About 750 years ago, an average size field of wheat could feed five people for a year. Today, in a developed country, the same field can feed between thirty and fifty people and also supply enough seed to sow for the next crop!

\* \* \*

What do you get when you cross a cow with an American buffalo? The beefalo, of course! They breed this animal to produce more meat and help world food population.

## Which is correct?

1. a) There are more people than sheep in Australia.
   b) There are more sheep than kangaroos in Australia.
   c) There are more sheep than people in Australia.

2. a) There is no such animal as a beefalo.
   b) The beefalo comes from Australia and Cyprus.
   c) The beefalo is a cross between a cow and a buffalo.

3. a) An average size field can feed from 30 to 50 people for a year.
   b) An average size field can feed a family of five for a year.
   c) An average size field can feed 750 people for a year.

# Listen & Understand

**1.** a    b    c

**2.** a    b    c

**3.** a    b    c

**4.** a    b    c

**5.**

Listen and write down:
a)  what time she gets up
b)  how she gets to work
c)  where she works

# Partner Practice

—When are you going on vacation?
—In **June.**
—Where are you going?
— To **Canada.**
—How are you going?
—By **plane.**

*Now practice with a friend. You can say anything you like in place of* **June,**
**Canada** *and* **plane.**

—All-American Airlines. May I help you?
—Yes, I have a reservation for Flight 774 on Monday to Los Angeles.
  I want to change it to a later date please.
—What day and time?
—**Saturday the tenth at 3:40 p.m.**
— Okay, that's Flight 786.
— Thank you.

1.                          2.                          3.

Sunday **11**               Friday **4**               Wednesday **2**

plane - 10:30 in morning    plane - 9:50 in morning     plane - 3:45 in afternoon

| MEMORY BANK | 1. first | 2. second | 3. third |
| --- | --- | --- | --- |
| | 4. fourth | 5. fifth | 6. sixth |
| | 7. seventh | 8. eighth | 9. ninth |
| | 10. tenth | | |

—**Please open the window.**
—But I've already **opened** it.
—When?
—I **opened** it five minutes ago!

1. Please vacuum your room.

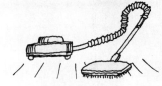

2. Please wash the floor.

3. Please wax the car.

4. Please iron my dress.

5. Please close the back door.

6. Please finish your homework.

7. Please empty the trash.

—Have you waxed the floors yet?
—No, I haven't, but I'm going to wax them tomorrow.

1. Have you washed the dishes yet?

2. Have you watered the flowers yet?

3. Have you polished your shoes yet?

4. Have you cleaned the closets yet?

5. Have you ironed the clothes yet?

6. Have you called Dick and Dot yet?

7. Have you emptied the wastebaskets yet?

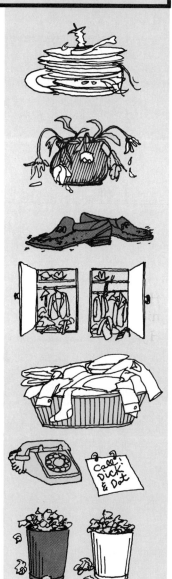

Mr. and Mrs. Walker are on vacation. Their children, Tom and Judy, have stayed at home. Mr. Walker has called them on the telephone. Mrs. Walker is telling him what to say.

—Hello, Tom? This is your father.

—Ask him if he has studied every day.

—Have you studied every day?

—Ask if Judy has cooked dinner every night.

—Has Judy cooked dinner every night?

—Ask if he has waxed the floors.

—Have you waxed the floors?

—Ask if he has cleaned the closets.

—Have you cleaned the closets?

—Ask if Judy has ironed the clothes.

—Has Judy ironed the clothes?

—Ask if she has watered the flowers.

—Has she watered the flowers?

—Ask if he has emptied the trash.

—Have you emptied the trash?

—Ask if he has walked the dog.

—Have you walked the dog?
What?

—What did he say?

—They haven't!

—Well, ask why not!

—Why not?

—Well, what did he say?

—They're taking a vacation too!

# Read & Understand

A HELPING HAND

Peter is very tired. He has just helped his mother in her new house. He says, "Mother, I've finished."

"But have you carried in all the boxes?"

"Yes, I have, Mother. I carried them in this morning."

"Have you washed all the windows?"

"Yes, Mother. I washed them at ten o'clock."

"Have you moved all the furniture?"

"YES, Mother. I have moved all the furniture. I have also emptied all the wastebaskets, and I have cleaned all the closets. I have waxed all the floors. I have worked all day."

"Wonderful, Peter. Now, can you do just one more thing . . .?"

"Oh, no. I have finished, Mother. Finished!"

"Oh, well," his mother says. "I guess I can do it myself."

"What?" asks Peter.

"Eat this beautiful cake I've just baked!"

1. How has Peter helped his mother today? He has carried in . . .
2. Why do you think Peter says "I have finished, mother!"?

# Conversations

BOB: Hi, Glenn.

GLENN: Hi, Bob. Mary has just phoned me.

BOB: What did she want?

GLENN: She has just moved, and she wants us to help.

BOB: Where's her new house?

GLENN: On $\begin{cases} \text{Green Street.} \\ \text{Borden Avenue.} \end{cases}$

BOB: This side of the bridge?

GLENN: No, the $\begin{cases} \text{first} \\ \text{second} \end{cases}$ street after the bridge.

BOB: What does she want us to do?

GLENN: $\begin{cases} \text{Paint the bedrooms.} \\ \text{Wax all the floors.} \end{cases}$

BOB: Oh no! I $\begin{cases} \text{painted the bedrooms} \\ \text{waxed the floors} \end{cases}$ in her old house!

GLENN: She wants us to $\begin{cases} \text{clean the closets} \\ \text{move the furniture} \end{cases}$ , too.

BOB: Sorry, I can't come.

GLENN: Are you sure? Mary has baked $\begin{cases} \text{a cake} \\ \text{chicken} \end{cases}$ for lunch.

BOB: Oh, maybe I *can* come!

# Career Corner

*Roger Harris is a zoologist — an expert on animal life. Career Corner is interviewing him.*

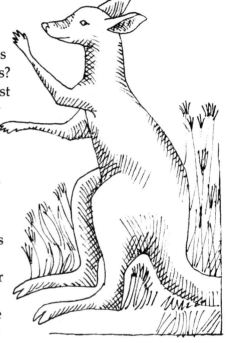

**CC**  Why do you find animals so fascinating, Dr. Harris?

**RH**  Many animals behave just like humans. They show their emotions even though they can't talk. Dogs wag their tails to show they are happy, for example. Cats don't *ever* wag their tails.

**CC**  So animals use their tails differently?

**RH**  Oh, yes. Horses use their tails to keep flies away. Some animals even store food in their tails. Sheep in the African and Asian deserts have long tails. When their isn't enough food, they can live off the fat that is stored in their tails.

**CC**  Is it true that some animals use their tails to fight?

**RH**  Yes, when the kangaroo fights, it stands on its tail and fights with its back legs. It uses its tail like a third leg.

**CC**  What about other animals?

**RH**  Well, a monkey uses its tail like a third arm. It holds on to trees and vines with its tail. Boa constrictors also hang by their tails.

**CC**  Oh, I don't like snakes!

**RH**  Most people don't like snakes, but they are really fascinating.

# Picture This!

Work in small groups. Use your imagination as you answer the questions. Then write about the picture on your own.

1. How did the dog fall into the river?
2. Which river is it? Which country is it in?
3. Who has the dog in his hand? Who called the police?
4. Do you think the dog's owner is in the photo? Which person is it?
5. Why is the young woman climbing down the bridge?
6. Pretend you're one of the people in the picture. Tell your story.

# To Everything There Is a Season

To everything there is a season, and a time
   to every purpose under the heaven:
A time to be born, and a time to die . . .
A time to weep, and a time to laugh . . .
A time to mourn, and a time to dance . . .
A time to get, and a time to lose . . .
A time to keep silence, and a time to speak . . .
A time to love, and a time to hate . . .
A time of war, and a time of peace.

*Ecclesiastes 3:1*

# Fast Track: *Read and Find Out*

## BUSINESS AND INDUSTRY

The oldest company on record is the Faversham Oyster Company of Great Britain. It started in 1189.

* * *

Governments and companies sell shares and raise money at stock exchanges. The oldest stock exchange in the world is at Amsterdam. It started in 1602.

* * *

Over thirty companies in the world make money from oil. The biggest producers are Saudi Arabia, USSR, USA, United Arab Emirates and Nigeria. Oil makes up one quarter of all world trade.

* * *

Exxon, a giant oil company in New York, earns more money in a year than many countries. Recently, it earned approximately $100,000 million — the same as the national income of Belgium.

**Which is correct?**

1. a) One of the oldest companies of the world started in Belgium.
   b) Exxon is one of the oldest companies in the world.
   c) One of the oldest companies in the world started in Great Britain.

2. a) Amsterdam has the oldest government in the world.
   b) Amsterdam has the oldest stock exchange in the world.
   c) Amsterdam has the oldest company in the world.

3. a) Oil produces 25% of all world trade,
   b) Oil is produced in 25% of all the countries of the world.
   c) Oil production started in Amsterdam in 1602.

# Pronunciation

I.
| | | | |
|---|---|---|---|
| he | cheap | green | teach |
| sleep | tea | teeth | piece |
| cream | really | people | engineer |
| these | eat | beach | please |
| jeans | hear | see | coffee |

There were many people at the beach today.

He is an engineer.

Please teach me these songs.

I want a piece of cake and tea with cream.

My grandfather's new teeth really look cheap!

II.
| | | | |
|---|---|---|---|
| eggs | best | well | friend |
| help | head | bread | breakfast |
| guess | instead | lesson | lettuce |
| ready | many | sweater | dead |
| jelly | bed | red | wet |

My best friend helps me with my lessons.

I like bread and jelly for breakfast.

Susan likes lettuce and egg sandwiches for breakfast.

I'm going to wear my red sweater to school.

I'm not going to the movies; I'm going to bed early instead.

III. Please put the cream, coffee, eggs and bread on the table.

Do you like my new jeans and sweater?

Please help me make eggs for breakfast.

Did you sleep well last night?

My little sister eats lettuce and jelly sandwiches!

Do you drink coffee, tea or milk for breakfast?

I was walking in the rain; my head is wet.

Please eat this piece of bread instead of that piece of cake.

# Partner Practice

—Where's Steven?
—He's at home, working.
—What's he doing?
—He's **washing the windows.**

1. **mowing the lawn**

2. **weeding the garden**

3. **cleaning the attic**

4. **sweeping the basement**

5. **repairing the car**

6. **fixing the TV**

—The Changs have moved to a new house.
—Really? Where?
—I don't know, exactly—**on the coast** somewhere.

1. **on the lake**

2. **in the mountains**

3. **in the woods**

4. **in the valley**

5. **in the suburbs**

6. **in the city**

| Can you **swim**? |  | Yes, I can.<br>No, I can't. |
| Could you **swim** last year? | | Yes, I could.<br>No, I couldn't. |

1.

2.

3.

4.

5.

6.

7.

8.

9.

**MEMORY BANK**

| | | |
|---|---|---|
| 1. dance | 2. play tennis | 3. cook |
| 4. skate | 5. sing | 6. play the piano |
| 7. type | 8. play chess | 9. speak English |

—Can you come to the movies today?
—No, I can't. I have to **clean the attic**.

1.

2.

3.

4.

5.

6.

—Why couldn't you come to the movies yesterday?
—I had to **mow the lawn**.

1.

2.

3.

4.

5.

6.

**MEMORY BANK**

| | | |
|---|---|---|
| 1. wash the windows | 2. fix the TV | 3. sweep the basement |
| 4. repair the car | 5. study | 6. weed the garden |
| 1. do the dishes | 2. type | 3. iron the clothes |
| 4. paint the bedroom | 5. vacuum | 6. wax the floors |

—Do you have to fix the **chair**?
—No, my father has already fixed **it**.

1.  2.  3.  4.

5.  6.  7.  8.

—Do you have to repair the **suitcase**?
—Yes, I do. My father hasn't repaired **it** yet.

1.  2.  3.  4.

5.  6.  7.  8.

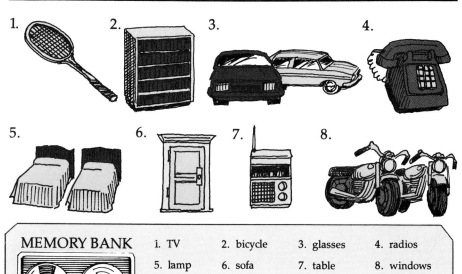

| MEMORY BANK | i. TV | 2. bicycle | 3. glasses | 4. radios |
| | 5. lamp | 6. sofa | 7. table | 8. windows |
| | 1. racket | 2. bookcase | 3. cars | 4. telephone |
| | 5. beds | 6. door | 7. radio | 8. motorcycles |

# Read & Understand

## DREAM HOUSES

I remember the time we were planning our first house. First we had to choose a place to live. Did we want to live in the city, or in the suburbs? Did we want a house in the valley, or in the mountains? In the woods, or on the lake, or on the coast?

Then we had to decide how many rooms we wanted. We needed a lot of new furniture. We wanted a nice yard, too. Our "dream house" was much too expensive. We had to save a lot more money. We still live in our little apartment.

*Which of these houses is your "dream house?" Why?*

# Conversations

MR. BEAN:   Well, hello! I haven't talked to you for ages!

MR. WEST:   Yes, at least $\begin{cases} \text{two years!} \\ \text{six months!} \end{cases}$

MR. BEAN:   Do you still live in the city?

MR. WEST:   No, I live $\begin{cases} \text{on the coast} \\ \text{in the suburbs} \\ \text{on the lake} \end{cases}$ now.

MR. BEAN:   Have you rented an apartment?

MR. WEST:   No, we own a house now.

MR. BEAN:   A big one?

MR. WEST:   Not really. $\begin{cases} \text{Six} \\ \text{Two} \\ \text{Three} \end{cases}$ bedrooms and a $\begin{cases} \text{study.} \\ \text{playroom.} \\ \text{dining room.} \end{cases}$

MR. BEAN:   Don't you miss the $\begin{cases} \text{theater?} \\ \text{restaurants?} \\ \text{concerts?} \end{cases}$

MR. WEST:   Yes, I do, but we often drive in from the $\begin{cases} \text{coast.} \\ \text{suburbs.} \\ \text{lake.} \end{cases}$

MR. BEAN:   How's the family?

MR. WEST:   Oh, just fine.

MR. BEAN:   Glad to hear it. Well, let's get together soon.

MR. WEST:   Yes, let's. See you later.

MR. BEAN:   Bye.

MR. WEST:   Hmm . . . who *was* that?

# Career Corner

*Tom Bolton is an anthropologist. He has spent many years studying the Maori natives of New Zealand. Career Corner is interviewing him.*

**CC** How far back do the Maori in New Zealand go?

**TB** Well, they arrived some time in the fourteenth century.

**CC** What sort of people were they?

**TB** They were fighters, mainly. They were very brave. There's a story — we don't know if it's true or not. But there's a story about the Maori fighting Captain Cook. When Cook and his men were just about beaten, the Maori sent food to them so they could fight longer!

**CC** Was the land and climate the same then?

**TB** Yes, it was. The earliest settlers of New Zealand found a subtropical climate. They found beautiful mountains, lakes, forests, and fiords.

**CC** Didn't the Maori have a lot of gods?

**TB** Yes. The most powerful god was called Io. The Maoris also believed in the laws of Tapu. Tapu protected the chief and the lands of the tribe. If you broke the Tapu, they believed, you'd be punished.

**CC** Tapu?

**TB** Yes, that's right. It's the same as the English word *taboo*, which means something forbidden.

# Picture This!

Work in small groups. Use your imagination as you answer the questions. Then write about the picture on your own.

1. What happened in this picture?
2. How many people are helping the person on the ground?
3. What vehicles do you see?
4. What will happen next?
5. Why do you think there is a helicopter at the scene?

# The Lion and the Mouse

One day, the Lion was sleeping. The Mouse ran across the Lion's paws. The Lion woke up, and was angry. He grabbed the Mouse and opened his huge jaws.

"Don't eat me!" the Mouse begged. "Please! I'm sorry. Let me go, and maybe someday, I can help you in some way." The Lion laughed. "How could you help *me*?" But he let the Mouse go.

Some time later, the Mouse heard the Lion roaring angrily. The Mouse ran to see what was wrong. The Lion was caught in a hunter's net.

The Mouse said, "Don't worry. I'll get you out of there." He began to nibble on the net. He nibbled and nibbled, and finally, there was a hole in the net. The Lion squeezed through the hole. He was free again. "Thank you, Mouse." "You're welcome, Lion. And let this be a lesson to you."

*What is the moral of this fable?*

# Fast Track: *Read and Find Out*

## FOOD AND DRINK

Calories show the energy content of different foods. We all need a certain amount each day to make our bodies work properly. Unfortunately, people in Europe and the US now eat about 20 times as much sugar and at least five times as much fat as they did in 1800. This may have something to do with the increase in heart disease in Western countries.

*   *   *

For wedding feasts, the Bedouin people sometimes prepare a meal of stuffed roast camel. First, they stuff a fish with eggs. Then they put the fish inside a chicken. They put the chicken inside a whole roast sheep. Then, finally, they put all of this inside a cooked camel!

*   *   *

The avocado contains 165 calories for every 100 grams of fruit. This is more than eggs or milk. It also contains twice as much protein as milk and has more vitamin A, B and C.

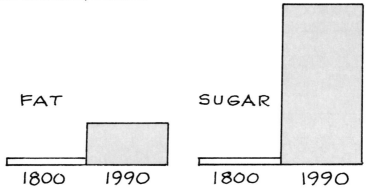

**Which is correct?**

1. a) Calories show the fat content of food.
   b) Calories show the sugar content of food.
   c) Calories show the energy content of food.

2. a) People eat more sugar in Europe than in the US.
   b) People in Europe and the US eat more sugar than ever before.
   c) People eat more fat in the US than in Europe.

3. a) The avocado weighs 100 grams.
   b) The avocado is a fruit.
   c) An avocado fruit has 165 calories.

# Listen & Understand

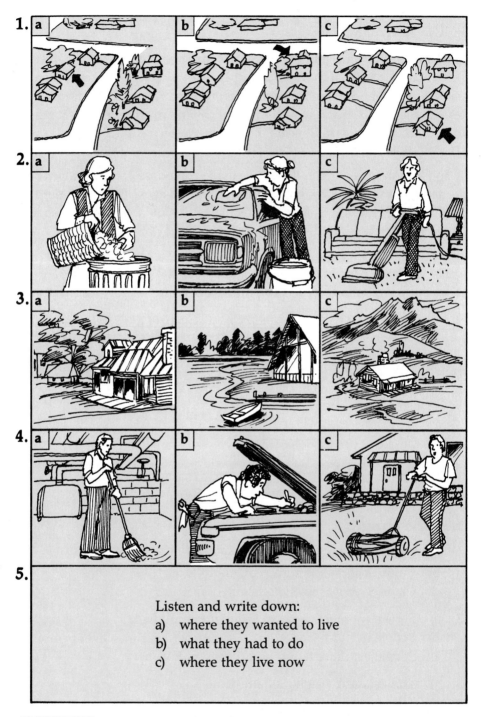

5.

Listen and write down:
a)  where they wanted to live
b)  what they had to do
c)  where they live now

# 6

Look at this great souvenir!
Six-fifty.
How much did it cost?
DALLAS
TOUR USA
State Fair
Cotton Bowl
EAST
NORTH
NORTH

# Partner Practice

—**What's he** doing?
—**He's** taking a picture of **his mother.**

1. What are they doing?

2. What's she doing?

3. What are you doing?

4. What's he doing?

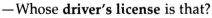

—Whose **driver's license** is that?
—Can you guess?
—Um . . . Is it **Tom's**?
—Right! It's **his!**

1. **passport (hers)**

2. **student card (his)**

3. **baby picture (hers)**

4. **charge card (his)**

*What does he do every day?*
*What does she do every day?*

1.

2.

3.

4.

*What do they do every day?*

1.

2.

3.

4.

1. How much did they bet?  They bet a dollar.

2. How much did he bet?  He bet a nickel.

3. What did she hit him with?  She hit him with an umbrella.

4. Where did she hit him?  She hit him in the mouth.

5. What did he cut?  He cut his cheek.

6. What did she cut?  She cut her hair.

7. How much did it cost?  It cost 75 cents.

8. How much did they cost?  They cost ten dollars.

9. Where did he put the photo?  He put it in his wallet.

10. Where did she put her watch? She put it in her briefcase.

| Did he bet a nickel? |  | No, he didn't bet a nickel.<br>He bet a quarter. |

1. Did he cut his finger?

2. Did she put it in her wallet?

3. Did it cost a dollar?

4. Did she hit him in the nose?

| Do you know how much it cost? |  | Yes, it cost five hundred dollars. |

1. Do you know where she hit him?

2. Do you know where she put the dog?

3. Do you know how much they bet?

4. Do you know what she cut?

# Read & Understand

HORSE SENSE

An American millionaire enjoyed photography. He had many kinds of cameras. He liked to take his cameras to the racetrack when his own horses were running.

One evening when he was developing his film, he saw something interesting. He called a friend to tell him about it. The millionaire said that a horse lifted all its legs at the same time when it galloped. "I don't believe it," his friend answered. "Do you want to bet?" asked the millionaire. "It'll cost you $500 to find out who is right."

The next day the two friends were at the racetrack. The millionaire put twenty-four cameras around the track. He tied a string to each camera. One of the millionaire's horses galloped around the track. When it passed a camera, its legs cut the string, and the camera clicked a picture. You can see some of the pictures here.

Who won the bet?

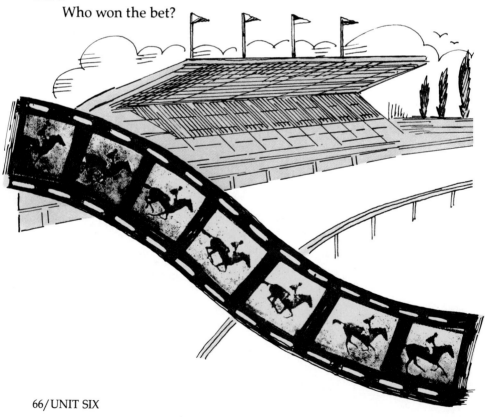

# Conversations

| | |
|---|---|
| PHOTOGRAPHER: | $\begin{cases} \text{Good morning.} \\ \text{Hello.} \\ \text{Good afternoon.} \end{cases}$ |
| MR. MILAN: | $\begin{cases} \text{Good morning.} \\ \text{Hello.} \\ \text{Good afternoon.} \end{cases}$ I want a picture of myself. |

PHOTOGRAPHER: Tomorrow at $\begin{cases} \text{2:15?} \\ \text{4:30?} \end{cases}$

MR. MILAN: No, that's too $\begin{cases} \text{early.} \\ \text{late.} \end{cases}$

PHOTOGRAPHER: How about Wednesday, then?

MR. MILAN: $\begin{cases} \text{No, I have to go to the doctor.} \\ \text{Sorry, that's my day off.} \end{cases}$ Can you do it right now?

PHOTOGRAPHER: Sure. What's the photo for?

MR. MILAN: $\begin{cases} \text{A passport.} \\ \text{My mother's birthday.} \end{cases}$

PHOTOGRAPHER: $\begin{cases} \text{Oh, you can have it in an hour.} \\ \text{It's going to be ready next week.} \end{cases}$

MR. MILAN: How much do six copies cost?

PHOTOGRAPHER: $\begin{cases} \text{They cost four dollars.} \\ \text{They cost from ten to twenty dollars.} \end{cases}$

MR. MILAN: Okay, what do you want me to do?

PHOTOGRAPHER: $\begin{cases} \text{Just stand here, please.} \\ \text{Sit on that chair, please.} \end{cases}$ And say, "cheese."

MR. MILAN: Cheeeeeese!

# Career Corner

*Elizabeth Boulder is a geologist — an expert on rocks. She is studying volcanoes in Hawaii. Career Corner is interviewing her.*

**CC** What is a volcano, exactly?

**EB** A volcano is a mountain made by hot, melted rock from inside the earth. The melted rock, called lava, bursts through the surface of the earth. Powdered ashes and small rocks are thrown into the air when the burst, or eruption, takes place. The hot lava builds up the cone-shaped mountain we call a volcano.

**CC** But it isn't as hot on the surface as under the ground, is it?

**EB** No. That's why the lava cools down and forms rock again.

**CC** And the new rock can make a volcano with a crater in it?

**EB** That's right. Mauna Loa and Kilauea, on the island of Hawaii, are still growing. Kilauea had a big eruption in 1960, and Mauna Loa has smaller eruptions quite often.

**CC** Are there volcanoes on all the islands of Hawaii?

**EB** Mauna Loa and Kilauea are the only active volcanoes, but all of Hawaii was formed by volcanoes. The Hawaiian Islands are the tops of volcanic mountains.

# Picture This!

Work in small groups. Use your imagination as you answer the questions. Then write about the picture on your own.

1. What is happening here?
2. What are the people watching?
3. How many houses are on fire?
4. How do you think the fire started?
5. What will happen next?

# Sunning

Old Dog lay in the summer sun
Much too lazy to rise and run.
He flapped an ear
At a buzzing fly.
He winked a half opened
Sleepy eye.
He scratched himself
On an itching spot,
As he dozed on the porch
Where the sun was hot.
He whimpered a bit
From force of habit
While he lazily dreamed
Of chasing a rabbit.
But Old Dog happily lay in the sun
Much too lazy to rise and run.

*James S. Tippett*

# Fast Track: *Read and Find Out*

## CITIES

In 1626 a Dutchman bought an island in America from some local Indians. He gave them some cloth and beads worth about $24. He had bought Manhattan, now one of the most crowded and expensive islands in the world. He named his town New Amsterdam. Later they changed the name to New York.

\* \* \*

Archaeologists believe that Jericho in Jordan is the oldest continuously inhabited place in the world. There were as many as 3,000 people living there as early as 9,800 years ago.

\* \* \*

We know the capital of Thailand is Bangkok. The Thais call it Krung Thep for short. The full name has 167 letters and means "The City of Gods, the Great City, the Residence of the Emerald Buddha, the Impregnable City of God Indira, the Grand Capital of the World Endowed with Nine Precious Gems, the Happy City Abounding in an Enormous Royal Palace Which Resembles the Heavenly Abode Where the Reincarnated God Reigns, a City Given by Indira and Built by Vishnukarn."

## Which is correct?

1.  a)  You can buy Manhattan for $24.
    b)  A man from Holland bought Manhattan.
    c)  Indians bought Manhattan from a Dutchman.

2.  a)  Almost 10,000 years ago there were 3,000 people living in Jericho.
    b)  Archaeologists lived in Jericho 9,800 years ago.
    c)  Archaeologists have inhabited Jericho continuously for almost 10,000 years.

3.  a)  Krung Thep is not the capital city of Thailand.
    b)  Bangkok is not the capital city of Thailand.
    c)  Krung Thep and Bangkok are the same city.

# Pronunication

I.

| time | night | like | ride |
|------|-------|------|------|
| dry | iron | side | diet |
| miles | light | prize | sigh |
| why | pilot | type | try |
| my | kind | five | license |

I'm trying to get a driver's license.

Jane is on a diet — she sighs a lot!

Dan is a pilot. He flies 2,000 miles every week.

Put the prize inside this box.

Please dry my shirts and iron them tonight.

II.

| milk | film | dinner | English |
|------|------|--------|---------|
| bridge | fifth | ship | guitar |
| wrist | women | trick | sink |
| fix | sit | miss | sing |
| win | hit | live | kitchen |

I like to play the guitar and sing in English.

Do you live across the big bridge?

We're going to see a film after dinner.

Can you fix the kitchen sink for me?

My mother hit a bus, but she missed the tree behind it!

III.

Did Mary win the first prize last night?

I like to ride my bike across the bridge.

The women in the kitchen are on a diet.

Ben hit Dick on his wrist, and now he can't play the guitar.

Why did you type this letter five times?

We're sitting in the kitchen, drinking milk and singing songs.

What are you reading?

No, I like non-fiction.

A spy novel. Do you like this type of book?

GRAND CANYON

TOUR USA

# Partner Practice

—I have just read an interesting travel book.
—What was it about?
—A journey to **Africa** in **1954**.

1. **Australia**   1948
3. **China**   1789

2. **India**   1970
4. **Scandinavia** 1972

—Are you reading a good book?
—Yes, I am.
—What's it about?
—**A bank robbery**.
—Oh, you like **police stories**, don't you?

1. **Cowboys and Indians**
   **westerns**

2. **A woman in love**
   **romance novels**

3. **Men from Mars**
   **science fiction**

4. **A spy in Berlin**
   **mysteries**

5. **Europe in 1812**
   **history**

6. **Elvis Presley**
   **biographies**

*What did they do yesterday?*

1. Where did she sleep?  She slept on the sofa.

2. Where did he sleep?  He slept on the rug.

3. What did Farmer Black keep?  He kept chickens.

4. What did Farmer Brown keep?  He kept pigs.

5. Where did he leave her?  He left her at the racetrack.

6. Where did he leave his car?  He left it at the hotel.

7. How did she feel?  She felt upset.

8. What did she mean? She meant "no!"

9. Who did she meet?  She met Paul.

10. What did she read?  She read a magazine.

Did she sleep on the sofa?  No, she didn't sleep on the sofa.
She slept on the rug.

1. Did he mean "yes?"

2. Did she feel happy?

3. Did he leave her at the hotel?

4. Did she meet her brother?

5. Did they keep pigs?

6. Did she read a book?

—When is she going to meet Mark?
—Oh, she has already met him.

1. When is she going to read that book?
2. When is she going to leave the hotel?
3. When is she going to sleep on the new bed?

# Read & Understand

## SCIENCE FICTION

Have you read any books by Jules Verne, the French author? He was a man who dreamed about fantastic journeys. In 1865 he wrote a book about a journey to the moon. The spaceship he created was very comfortable. The passengers, two Americans and one Frenchman, kept chickens in the ship for food! They slept on good beds and cooked their meals on a gas stove. They reached the moon 97 hours, 13 minutes, and 20 seconds after they had left the earth. When they landed on the moon they made a mistake, and couldn't leave the spaceship. This was a good thing, since they had no space suits!

Verne's books are called science fiction. In his time, people felt Verne's stories were impossible dreams. But one hundred years later, men were walking on the moon!

1. Who was Jules Verne?
2. Why do you think he liked to write about fantastic journeys?
3. When did he write about a journey to the moon?
4. What was the spaceship like?
5. How is this spaceship different from real spaceships?
6. What would happen if the passengers left the spaceship?
7. Why did people feel like Verne's stories were impossible dreams?

# Conversations

PETER: Let's buy Antonio a book for his birthday.

MARIA: Good idea. How about a { western? / mystery? / biography? }

PETER: Well, I think he only likes { history. / police stories. / romance novels. }

MARIA: Umm, how about magazines instead?

PETER: No, he { always / usually } reads them at the library.

MARIA: I know he likes { sports. / photography. / music. }

PETER: Then how about { some film? / a book on baseball? / a songbook? }

MARIA: I can't decide.

PETER: { He'll like anything. / Let's just give him a card. / Let's just give him some money. }

MARIA: I guess you're right.

PETER: Of course. I'm *always* right!

# Career Corner

*Paul Porter works for the United Nations. He's an agronomist. Career Corner is interviewing him.*

**CC** What sort of farming do you specialize in?

**PP** Well, mainly groundnuts.

**CC** Groundnuts?

**PP** Oh, you probably call them peanuts.

**CC** Oh, I love peanuts! But aren't they from North America?

**PP** Some, yes. But peanuts grow all over the world these days. Originally, Spanish explorers discovered peanuts when they were looking for gold in South America. They weren't very impressed by the nuts, but they took them back to Europe anyhow.

**CC** Are peanuts an important cash crop?

**PP** Yes. In the United States, peanuts are grown on large plantations. In 1987, over 44 million pounds of peanuts were grown!

**CC** Do they grow easily?

**PP** Fairly easily. They need a good climate with moderate rainfall, much sunshine, and warm temperatures.

**CC** How long does it take them to grow?

**PP** Between 130 and 150 days. First, small yellow flowers appear after a month. Then come the seed pods. The pods bury themselves in the ground. The nuts themselves grow under the ground.

**CC** So that's why you call them groundnuts!

**PP** Right!

# Picture This!

Work in small groups. Use your imagination as you answer the questions. Then write about the picture on your own.

1. Who are these people?
2. How old are they?
3. Are they related to each other?
4. Where do they live?
5. These people are making pottery. What do you think they will do with the pottery? Will they use it in their home? Will they sell it?
6. Have you ever made pottery? If not, would you like to try this craft?

# Belling the Cat

Once, some mice were frightened of a cat that lived in their house. The mice decided to hold a meeting and talk over the problem.

"That cat is always sneaking up and surprising me," said the first mouse. "Right!" said the second mouse. "We have to run for our lives every day." "I have an idea," said the third mouse. "Let's tie a bell around the cat's neck. Then we can hear him coming, and have plenty of time to run and hide."

The mice agreed it was a great idea. They got a bell and a piece of ribbon. "Now," said the first mouse. "Who is going to tie the bell on the cat?"

"Not I!" said the second mouse.

"Not I!" said the third mouse.

None of them was brave enough to bell the cat.

*What is the moral of this fable?*

# Fast Track: *Read and Find Out*

## COMMUNICATIONS

Nowadays satellites orbit the earth. Television can reach a potential audience of about 2.5 billion people. The whole world can watch the Olympic Games at the same time.

*   *   *

When *The Times* newspaper reported Lord Nelson's victory over the French at the Battle of Trafalgar in 1805, the news took two and a half weeks to reach London. Then the same newspaper, 164 years later, showed pictures of the first men on the moon a few hours after the landing.

*   *   *

Men have talked to each other directly between the earth and the moon—a distance of 400,000 kilometers. Now scientists have sent a powerful radio signal into space. They expect it to take 24,000 years to reach its destination, a group of stars. That's a long time to wait for a reply!

### Which is correct?

1.  a) People all over the world can watch television at the same time because of Nelson's victory over the French.
    b) If everyone in the world had a TV, about 2.5 billion people could watch the Olympic Games at the same time because of satellites that orbit the earth.
    c) A potential audience of about 2.5 billion people can orbit the earth on satellites.

2.  a) It took two and a half weeks for Nelson to defeat the French at the Battle of Trafalgar in 1805.
    b) Nelson read about the Battle of Trafalgar two and a half weeks later in *The Times* newspaper.
    c) Nelson defeated the French at the Battle of Trafalgar.

3.  a) The first men landed on the moon in 1805.
    b) The first moon landing was in 1969.
    c) In 1969, people landed on the moon for the first time.

# Listen & Understand

1. a  b  c

2. a  b  c

3. a  b  c

4. a  b  c

5.
Listen and write down:
a)  what she rented
b)  what she read
c)  who she met

# 8

FREMONT
Those hotels look expensive.
I hope they're not as expensive as they look.
LAS VEGAS
TOUR USA

# Partner Practice

—Are you going to the game?
—No, I've decided to stay home.
—Why?
—I'm going to **weed the garden**.

1. **build a bookcase**

2. **clean the basement**

3. **fix the refrigerator**

4. **iron the clothes**

—That **coffee** smells **wonderful**.
—Wait until you taste it.
—What do you mean?
—It tastes **wonderful**, too.

1.  delicious

2.  great

3.  marvelous

4.  strong

—Those **cookies** look **good**.
—Thanks.
  I hope they taste as **good** as they look.

1.  juicy

2.  light

3. sweet

4.  fresh

—What did he ask you to do?
—He asked me to **pay the bill**.

1.    2.    3.

—What did she ask Tom to do?
—She asked him to **buy some flowers**.

1.    2.    3.

4.    5.    6.

---

**MEMORY BANK**

| | | |
|---|---|---|
| 1. clean the files | 2. work overtime | 3. type some letters |
| 1. play the guitar | 2. close the window | 3. take some pictures |
| 4. weed the garden | 5. send a letter | 6. build a table |

1. What did she send?  She sent a letter.

2. What did he send?  He sent a postcard.

3. What did she build?  She built a birdhouse.

4. What did he build?  He built a bookcase.

5. Where did she spend her vacation?  She spent it on a lake.

6. Where did he spend his vacation?  He spent it in the mountains.

7. What did she shoot?  She shot a pineapple.

8. What did he shoot?  He shot a can.

9. What did she lose?  She lost her perfume.

10. What did he lose?  He lost his wallet.

| | | |
|---|---|---|
| **Did he build a bookcase?** |  | **No, he didn't build a bookcase. He built a birdhouse.** |

1. Did he send a letter?

2. Did he spend two dollars?

3. Did she shoot a can?

4. Did he lose his gloves?

—When **is he** going to **send the letter?**
—Oh, **he has** already **sent** it.

1. When is he going to build the bookcase?
2. When are you going to spend your birthday money?
3. When are they going to meet Charlie?
4. When is she going to shoot the picture?
5. When is he going to read the newspaper?

# Read & Understand

## ON VACATION

Dear Susan,

The weather is wonderful in Puerto Rico. The days are warm and sunny, but the nights are unusually cool. It seldom rains, and it never snows.

I spent a week at a little hotel on the coast. There was a beautiful garden and swimming pool. There was a beach, too. The hotel food was really delicious. My room and meals cost $120 a day.

After a big breakfast, I spent the morning on the beach. I met friends for lunch every day. After lunch, I usually slept for a few hours. Then I read by the pool and had a cool drink. After dinner, I usually walked on the beach.

I have already decided to come back to Puerto Rico again next year. Do you want to come too?

Love,
Gloria

# Conversations

MAX: Did you call the airport?

DORIS:
$\begin{cases} \text{Yes, I did.} \\ \text{No, I didn't.} \end{cases}$ I'm ready. Let's go.

MAX: What's the weather like now?

DORIS:
$\begin{cases} \text{It's snowing.} \\ \text{It's pouring.} \end{cases}$

MAX: Let's hope it's $\begin{cases} \text{sunny in Spain.} \\ \text{warm in Boston.} \end{cases}$

DORIS:
$\begin{cases} \text{It's always sunny there in the summer.} \\ \text{It's usually warm there in June.} \end{cases}$ Hurry *up*!

MAX: Are you taking $\begin{cases} \text{a raincoat?} \\ \text{an umbrella?} \\ \text{boots?} \end{cases}$

DORIS: Yes, I've already packed $\begin{cases} \text{it.} \\ \text{them.} \end{cases}$ Let's go.

MAX: Have you $\begin{cases} \text{locked all the windows?} \\ \text{left a note for the newspaper boy?} \end{cases}$

DORIS: Yes, I have. Let's *go*!

MAX: Do you have the $\begin{cases} \text{tickets?} \\ \text{passports?} \end{cases}$

DORIS: No, I lost them.

MAX: What?

DORIS: I'm only joking, Max. Let's GO!

# Career Corner

*Henry Harrison is the captain of the "Mississippi Queen." Career Corner is interviewing him.*

**CC**  Tell us about the "Mississippi Queen," Captain.

**HH**  Well, she's a paddle steamer. She is five decks high. There is a theater and a swimming pool on board.

**CC**  How many passengers can the ship take?

**HH**  There are cabins for 400 passengers and a crew of 100.

**CC**  And you go up and down the Mississippi?

**HH**  That's right.

**CC**  Just how long is the Mississippi?

**HH**  It's 2,348 miles long. It begins in Lake Itasca, Minnesota. It ends in the Gulf of Mexico.

**CC**  Is it the longest river in North America?

**HH**  No. The Missouri-Red Rock is longer. It flows into the Mississippi. There are more than 250 other rivers that join the Mississippi. So you could travel tens of thousands of miles and be on rivers the whole time.

**CC**  Well, thank you, Captain. This was a very interesting interview.

**HH**  You're welcome.

# Picture This!

Work in small groups. Use your imagination as you answer the questions.
Then write about the picture on your own.

1. Who are these people?
2. What does the man in the hat do?
3. Does the woman like the man in the hat?
4. What are they saying to each other?
5. Where are they?
6. What will happen next?

# I Have Lived and I Have Loved

I have lived and I have loved;
I have waked and I have slept;
I have sung and I have danced;
I have smiled and I have wept;
I have won and wasted treasure;
I have had my fill of pleasure;
And all these things were
    weariness,
And some of them were
    dreariness.
And all these things — but
    two things
Were emptiness and pain;
And Love — it was the best
    of them;
And Sleep — worth all the rest
    of them.

*Anonymous*

# Fast Track: *Read and Find Out*

## TRAVEL

The Romans built over 50,000 miles of roads in Europe and the Middle East. After their conquest of Britain, it took just about a week to get from London to Rome by horse.

\* \* \*

The first petroleum driven car was on the road in 1885. It had three wheels and its top speed was 10 miles per hour. Now, about a hundred years later, there are enough cars in the world for every tenth person. If all the cars in the world met in one great traffic jam, it would go around the world 34 times!

\* \* \*

The Concorde jet travels faster than the speed of sound. It flies between London and New York, a distance of 3,500 miles at a speed of 1,500 miles an hour in just about three hours.

**Which is correct?**

1.  a)  In Roman times it took about seven days to get from Rome to London.
    b)  Romans built roads from the Far East to the Middle East.
    c)  In Roman times it was about 50,000 miles from London to Rome by road.

2.  a)  In 1885, there were over 100 cars on the road.
    b)  There are enough cars for one in every ten people on earth.
    c)  People drive around the world 34 times in traffic jams.

3.  a)  It takes about three hours for supersonic planes to cross the Atlantic Ocean.
    b)  You cannot hear the Concorde because it flies faster than sound.
    c)  The distance from London to New York was 3,500 miles but now it is only 1,500 miles by Concorde.

# Pronunciation

I.  show      romance      home      toast
    comb      open      close      sofa
    radio      stove      photo      mow
    those      own      toe      boat

Please don't eat toast on the sofa.
Jack is taking photos at the disco.
Can you show me how to wear this comb in my hair?
How many times a day do you open and close your mouth?

II. shop      coffee      hot      jog
    walk      watch      closet      copy
    cough      often      cost      off
    foggy      strong      shot      lock

I often walk on the beach in foggy weather.
Let's stop for a hot cup of coffee.
How much did your jogging suit cost?
Listen! Did you hear a cough from inside the closet?

III. play      rain      shave      paint
    bake      weigh      sale      basement
    wait      race      mistake      space
    train      plate      lake      same

I had to wait in the rain for the train.
I made a mistake and put beans on his plate.
We painted the basement of our house by the lake.
The cake I baked weighs five pounds!

IV. jacket      taxi      pack      attic
    wax      ambulance      happy      track
    magazine      romance      cash      last
    paddle      glass      bad      dance

We waxed the dance floor today.
My sister spends all her cash on romance magazines.
The woman took a taxi to the race track.
Last week I found a terrific old jacket in our attic.

RODEO DR
CALIFORNIA REPUBLIC
City of Beverly Hills
Parking
WILSHIRE BLVD.
Did you buy anything on Rodeo Drive?
Yes, I bought *one* postcard!
LOS ANGELES
TOUR USA

# Partner Practice

—What does your new boss look like?
—She's **a tall, thin woman**. She's **young**, too.

1.        2.        3.        4.

—What did you decide to do at work today?
—I decided to **go on strike!**

1. ask for more pay

2. look for a new job

3. work overtime

4. learn how to type

5. hire a secretary

6. clean out my files

—What did she ask the children to do?
—She asked them to **wash the dishes.**

1.    2.    3.

4.    5.    6.

—Why can't we go?
—Betty wants us to **wash the car**.

1.    2.    3.

MEMORY BANK

| | | |
|---|---|---|
| 1. set the table | 2. wash the car | 3. clean the windows |
| 4. iron the clothes | 5. make the beds | 6. mow the lawn |
| 1. repair the car | 2. fix the TV | 3. sweep the basement |

1. What did they fight for?  They fought for more pay.

2. What did they fight for?  They fought for more coffee breaks.

3. What did he buy?  He bought a pair of glasses.

4. What did she buy?  She bought a pair of slacks.

5. What did she teach?  She taught chemistry.

6. What did he teach?  He taught typing.

7. What did he catch?  He caught the bus.

8. What did she catch?  She caught the train.

9. What did he think about?  He thought about his new farm.

10. What did she think about?  She thought about her new car.

*Pretend you own a cat. A friend gives you a dog for your birthday.*

1. Where did your friend buy the dog?

2. Did your mother think the dog was good or bad?

3. What did the cat and dog do?

4. What did you teach your new dog to do?

5. What did the dog catch one night?

6. What did your mother think about the dog *then*?

---

—**Wasn't he going to buy a new car?**
—**Yes, but he hasn't bought it yet.**

---

1. Wasn't she going to build a birdhouse?
2. Weren't you going to read this new book?
3. Weren't they going to send us some money?
4. Wasn't he going to sleep in the yard?

# Read & Understand

THE NEW JOB

Judy thought her new job was great, but on her first day, everything was wrong. First she slept late. Then she caught the wrong bus. She arrived at the factory at nine instead of eight-thirty. Her new boss was very angry. He taught her what to do in a hurry. All she had to do was watch a machine. It filled bottles with perfume. Then Judy pushed a button and sent the bottles to another worker.

At lunch, her boss asked her to buy him a sandwich. She bought a sandwich, but she dropped it and stepped on it! She bought another sandwich. Then she didn't have enough money for her own lunch. At the end of the afternoon, Judy felt very hungry and tired. She didn't want to see another bottle of perfume again in her life.

The next morning Judy arrived on time . . . and quit!

*Retell the story. The pictures will help you.*
*Why do you think Judy quit her job?*

# Conversations

INTERVIEWER: Good morning. What's your name, address and phone number, please?

JOB HUNTER: . . . .

INTERVIEWER: Do you have a job now?

JOB HUNTER: Yes, I'm a $\begin{cases} \text{secretary} \\ \text{typist} \\ \text{factory worker} \end{cases}$ now.

INTERVIEWER: How long have you worked as a $\begin{cases} \text{secretary?} \\ \text{typist?} \\ \text{factory worker?} \end{cases}$

JOB HUNTER: For $\begin{cases} \text{. . . years.} \\ \text{. . . weeks.} \\ \text{. . . months.} \end{cases}$

INTERVIEWER: Why do you want a new job?

JOB HUNTER: The one I have now $\begin{cases} \text{doesn't pay well.} \\ \text{isn't interesting.} \\ \text{is too far away from my home.} \end{cases}$

INTERVIEWER: We need a good secretary. Can you $\begin{cases} \text{take shorthand?} \\ \text{type?} \\ \text{file?} \end{cases}$

JOB HUNTER: Oh, yes. How much does this job pay?

INTERVIEWER: . . . dollars a $\begin{cases} \text{week.} \\ \text{month.} \\ \text{year.} \end{cases}$

JOB HUNTER: What are the hours? $\begin{cases} \text{Nine to five?} \\ \text{Eight to four?} \\ \text{Eight-thirty to four-thirty?} \end{cases}$

INTERVIEWER: That's right. And you get $\begin{cases} \text{one week} \\ \text{two weeks} \\ \text{three weeks} \end{cases}$ of vacation.

JOB HUNTER: Can I start right away?

INTERVIEWER: $\begin{cases} \text{You have to take a test first.} \\ \text{You have to see the boss first.} \\ \text{You have to fill out these papers first.} \end{cases}$

JOB HUNTER: Fine.

# Career Corner

*Abby Arnold works at a large zoo. She is a veterinarian. Her favorite animal is the koala bear. Career Corner is interviewing her.*

CC  Tell us about koala bears, Abby.

AA  They're short, fat little animals. They come from Australia. They look like toy bears.

CC  But they're not bears, are they?

AA  No, they're not. They're marsupials. Marsupials are animals with pouches. When a baby koala is born, it's no bigger than a bee. It has no hair, and it can't see. But it makes its way into the mother's pouch. If a baby doesn't find its way into the pouch, it dies.

CC  How long does the baby stay inside the pouch?

AA  From a few weeks up to six months.

CC  What happens when the baby koala leaves the pouch?

AA  After that, the baby likes to ride on its mother's back. Koalas live in eucalyptus trees. They sleep all day and eat at night. They eat about a pound of leaves every night!

CC  Are there many marsupials in the world?

AA  No, not many. Most of them like koalas and kangaroos live in or near Australia.

CC  Do people hunt koalas?

AA  Not any more. It's against the law, now.

CC  Good!

# Picture This!

Work in small groups. Use your imagination as you answer the questions. Then write about the picture on your own.

1. Who is the man in the uniform?
2. What is he holding?
3. Who is in the car?
4. What is the man saying?
5. Did the person in the car do something wrong?
6. What will happen next?

# The Crow and the Partridge

One day, a crow was flying across a road. She looked down and saw a partridge. The partridge was strutting along, looking very beautiful.

"Oh," thought the crow. "I wish I could walk as beautifully as the partridge." The crow flew down to the road and started walking behind the partridge. The crow tried to copy the partridge's wonderful strut.

The partridge turned around. "And just what do you think you're doing?" the partridge demanded.

"Don't be angry," replied the crow. "I'm just trying to learn to walk like you."

"Foolish bird!" answered the partridge. "You're a crow. Walk like a crow!"

But the crow didn't listen to good advice. She kept trying to strut like a partridge. She never did learn how to strut. And she forgot how to walk like a crow!

*What's the moral of this fable?*

# Fast Track: *Read and Find Out*

## MONEY

Coins and notes are not the only form of money. People have used teeth of animals, metal bracelets, shells, axe heads, blocks of salt, even blocks of tea. The word "cash" comes from an Indian word meaning "compressed tea." The word "salary" comes from the Latin word for "salt."

\* \* \*

When the price of buying things goes up, money becomes worthless. This is called inflation. After World War I, the German mark dropped in value from 81 marks to an American dollar to one million marks a dollar.

\* \* \*

Many governments take money from the salaries of their citizens. This is income tax. William Pitt, the Prime Minister of Great Britain introduced income tax in 1799 to pay for the war against Napoleon. The war ended almost 200 years ago, but income tax is still with us.

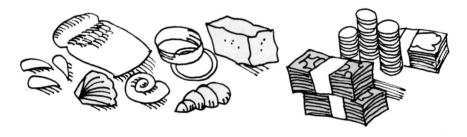

## Which is correct?

1. a) Coins and notes are the only forms of money.
   b) You can only buy compressed tea for cash.
   c) Money has many forms.

2. a) In an inflation prices usually go up and up.
   b) Inflation makes prices go down very quickly because money is worthless.
   c) After World War I you got 1,000,000 dollars for just one German mark.

3. a) Income tax ended over 150 years ago in Great Britain.
   b) We pay income tax to the government to fight Napoleon.
   c) We pay income tax from our salaries.

# Listen & Understand

**1.** a b c

**2.** a b c

**3.** a b c

**4.** a b c

**5.**

Listen and write down:
a) what she bought
b) what she taught
c) what she caught

# 10

It was a wonderful tour, wasn't it?
Yes, I really enjoyed it.
Let's stay in touch. Here's my address and phone number . . .
SAN FRANCISCO
TOUR USA

# Partner Practice

—Hello, **298-3394**.
—Hello. May I speak to John?
—I'm sorry. He's not at home.
—Where is he?
—He's at the **store**.

1. 944–3700

2. 242-2599

3. 964~6387

4. 251-4856

5. 246-2631

6. 275-8034

---

**MEMORY BANK**

1. library      2. beach

3. movies      4. factory

5. bank        6. driving range

—Was anybody in the **house**?
—No, but I think somebody was in the **garden**.

kitchen

1. living room

yard

2. garage

hall

3. classroom

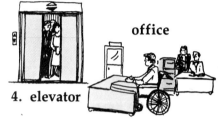

office

4. elevator

—There's something over there!
—Where? I can't see anything.
—Look, **next to that tree**!
—Oh, there's nothing there.

1. behind the fence

2. in front of the garage

3. near the back door

4. beside the chair

5. under the car

6. in the bathtub

1. What did he write?  He wrote a book.

2. What did she write?  She wrote a message.

3. Who did he speak to?  He spoke to a doctor.

4. Who did she speak to?  She spoke to a waiter.

5. What did he break?  He broke his arm.

6. What did she break?  She broke her leg.

7. What did he drive?  He drove a bus.

8. What did she drive?  She drove a taxi.

9. What did he choose for lunch?  He chose fish.

10. What did she choose for lunch?  She chose meat.

> —My mother wrote this book.
>
> —What? Who wrote it?
>
> —My mother did.

1. My grandfather spoke to my teacher.
2. My brother broke my bike.
3. My uncle drove to Mexico.
4. My aunt chose this dress.

> —Don't write that message.
>
> —But I have already written it.

1. Don't drive my car.
2. Don't break that egg.
3. Don't choose that perfume.
4. Don't speak to her.

> —Have you written to Pedro yet?
>
> —Yes, I wrote to him yesterday.

1. Have you driven your new car yet?
2. Have you chosen a new secretary yet?
3. Have you spoken to Ellen yet?
4. Have you broken that ugly dish yet?

| REMEMBER: | | | | | |
|---|---|---|---|---|---|
| I | write | I | wrote | I have | written |
| | drive | | drove | | driven |
| | break | | broke | | broken |
| | choose | | chose | | chosen |
| | speak | | spoke | | spoken |

# Read & Understand

Ted-

I thought I was going to be home now when I spoke to you last night, but I have just left for my mother's. Somebody stole her jewelry! I have to drive right over because she's very upset. I tried to call you, but your line was busy. You can call me at my mother's. Her number is 723-7693. Sorry to have missed you. Please choose another night for us to get together.

Karen

### TRUE OR FALSE?
1. Ted wrote a note to Karen.
2. Karen is not at home.
3. Ted and Karen had a date.
4. Karen has just left for her mother's.
5. Somebody stole her mother's car.
6. Karen didn't try to call Ted.
7. Karen's phone number is 723-7693.
8. Karen doesn't want to see Ted.

### ON YOUR OWN
Write a message. Tell why you're not at home. Tell where you are and when you are going to return. Leave the telephone number of the place where you are.

# Conversations

SOPHIE: Hello, 693-7723.

ALICE: Hello, Sophie? This is Alice.

SOPHIE: Hi, Alice. Have you spoken to Mike about tonight?

ALICE: Yes, I have. He wants to go to the {movies. / races.}

SOPHIE: Well, Dick wants to go to the {concert. / disco.}

ALICE: Who's going to choose, then?

SOPHIE: I think Mike is.

ALICE: Why?

SOPHIE: Because Dick doesn't have any money!

ALICE: I thought so. Well, can you and Dick pick us up?

SOPHIE: No, somebody stole his {truck. / car.}

ALICE: Oh no!

SOPHIE: Oh yes! And Dick was chasing the {truck, / car,} and broke his {arm. / leg.}

ALICE: Oh, that's too bad. Well, Mike and I can catch the {bus. / train.}

SOPHIE: Right. See you at {8:00 / 7:30} in front of the {movie theater. / racetrack.}

ALICE: {See you soon. / Bye.}

# Career Corner

*Rose Barry is a botanist — an expert on plants and the environment. Career Corner is interviewing her.*

CC   I understand that many trees are dying.

RB   That's right. There's a huge amount of pollution in the air. Pollution kills trees, plants, even animals.

CC   Where does the pollution come from?

RB   Well, some of it comes from factories. Some of it comes from cars and trucks.

CC   How does pollution spread?

RB   The wind carries it. It spreads it far away from the place where it began. When it rains, the pollution in the air comes back down. We call that acid rain.

CC   Why is acid rain a bad thing?

RB   Acid rain is killing whole forests. It's poisoning the soil. It's poisoning our lakes and rivers.

CC   Is acid rain really a serious problem?

RB   Absolutely. Some scientists believe that in twenty years all the great forests of the world may be dead.

# Picture This!

Work in small groups. Use your imagination as you answer the questions. Then write about the picture on your own.

*This is Speakers' Corner in Hyde Park, London. The speakers talk about whatever they want — war, religion, politics — just about anything can be heard at Speakers' Corner.*

1. Describe the speaker.
   What kind of person is he?
2. What do you think he's talking about?
3. Do you want to give a speech at Speakers' Corner? Why? What's the speech about?
4. Write your speech down, and deliver it to the class.

# Why Nobody Pets the Lion at the Zoo

The morning that the world began
The Lion growled a growl at Man.

And I suspect the Lion might
(If he'd been closer) have tried a bite.

I think that's as it ought to be
And not as it was taught to me.

I think the Lion has a right
To growl a growl and bite a bite.

And if the Lion bothered Adam,
He should have growled right back at 'im.

The way to treat a Lion right
Is growl for growl and bite for bite.

True, the Lion is better fit
For biting than for being bit.

But if you look him in the eye
You'll find the Lion's rather shy.

He really wants someone to pet him.
The trouble is: his teeth won't let him.

He has a heart of gold beneath
But the Lion just can't trust his teeth.

*John Ciardi*

# Fast Track: *Read and Find Out*

## LANGUAGES

People speak English as a first or second language in at least 45 countries. It is the language of international business and scientific conferences. Air traffic controllers use it worldwide. In all, about one third of the world speaks English.

\* \* \*

English has more words in it than any other language, about one million in all. Most people never use more than about 10,000 words.

\* \* \*

In the 1880s, a Pole by the name of Dr. Zamenhof invented an international language called Esperanto. He took words from many European languages in the hope that Esperanto would become the international language of Europe. The grammar is very simple. It takes about an hour to learn it, that's all!

**Which is correct?**
1. a)  About 30% of the world can speak some English.
   b)  Air traffic controllers never speak English.
   c)  Most people speak English as a third language.

2. a)  Most people use about one million words in their lifetime.
   b)  Most people use about 10,000 words.
   c)  The English language has too many words in it.

3. a)  A man from Poland invented Esperanto.
   b)  Esperanto is very complicated.
   c)  It takes about an hour to learn English if you know enough Esperanto.

# Pronunciation

**I.**

| | | | |
|---|---|---|---|
| use | juice | vac<u>uu</u>m | us<u>u</u>ally |
| y<u>ou</u> | m<u>u</u>sic | st<u>u</u>dent | interv<u>iew</u> |
| m<u>u</u>seum | s<u>u</u>re | <u>u</u>niform | bea<u>u</u>tiful |

The students wear blue uniforms.

I usually vacuum the rugs on Saturday.

There is a beautiful new museum in Washington, D.C.

Are you ready for your interview?

**II.**

| | | | |
|---|---|---|---|
| b<u>u</u>t | <u>u</u>mbrella | c<u>ou</u>sin | b<u>u</u>tton |
| s<u>u</u>mmer | st<u>u</u>dy | m<u>u</u>ch | l<u>u</u>nch |
| c<u>o</u>me | p<u>u</u>ddle | m<u>o</u>nth | s<u>o</u>metimes |
| s<u>u</u>nny | <u>u</u>ncle | l<u>o</u>ve | c<u>u</u>t |

Can you come and see us this summer?

It was sunny and warm the month of June.

My cousin and my uncle are coming for lunch.

The students have to study.

**III.**

| | | | |
|---|---|---|---|
| di<u>sc</u>u<u>ss</u> | <u>sc</u>ien<u>c</u>e | ba<u>s</u>ement | pa<u>ss</u>port |
| bo<u>ss</u> | de<u>c</u>ide | my<u>s</u>tery | con<u>c</u>ert |
| roman<u>c</u>e | cha<u>s</u>e | me<u>ss</u>age | offi<u>c</u>e |
| poli<u>c</u>e | a<u>ss</u>istant | expen<u>s</u>ive | <u>s</u>weetheart |

The assistant usually gets to the office before her boss.

Do you like mystery or romance novels?

We decided to clean the basement on Saturday.

The police have the man's passport.

**IV.**

| | | | |
|---|---|---|---|
| the<u>s</u>e | clo<u>s</u>et | choo<u>s</u>e | clothe<u>s</u> |
| lo<u>s</u>e | new<u>s</u>paper | bu<u>s</u>y | chee<u>s</u>e |
| no<u>s</u>e | plea<u>s</u>e | u<u>s</u>e | wood<u>s</u> |
| surpri<u>s</u>e | exerci<u>s</u>e | doe<u>s</u> | goe<u>s</u> |

The boys go to exercise class every week.

Please put these clothes in the closet.

Which newspaper did you choose?

Does she know about the surprise party?

# Index